Children's Authors

H. A. Rey

Cari Meister
ABDO Publishing Company

visit us at
www.abdopub.com

Published by ABDO Publishing Company, 4940 Viking Drive, Suite 622, Edina, Minnesota 55435. Copyright © 2001 Abdo Consulting Group, Inc., Pentagon Tower, P.O. Box 398166, Minneapolis, Minnesota 55439 USA. International copyrights reserved in all countries. No part of this book may be reproduced in any form without written permission from the publisher.

Printed in the United States.

Photos: Corbis (pages 7, 9, 11, 13, 15), Timepix (page 17), Houghton Mifflin (page 19), Bettmann (pages 5, 21)
Editors: Bob Italia, Tamara L. Britton, Kate A. Furlong, Christine Fournier
Art Direction: Neil Klinepier

Library of Congress Cataloging-in-Publication Data

Meister, Cari.
   H.A. Rey / Cari Meister.
     p. cm. -- (Children's authors. Set 2)
   Includes bibliographical references and index.
   ISBN 1-57765-481-1
   1. Rey, H.A. (Hans Augusto), 1898---Juvenile literature. 2. Authors, American--20th Century--Biography--Juvenile literature. 3. Illustrators--United States--Biography--Juvenile literature. 4. Children's literature--Authorship--Juvenile literature. 5. Illustration of books--Juvenile literature. [1. Rey, H.A. (Hans Augusto), 1898- 2. Authors, American. 3. Illustrators.] I. Title. II. Series.

PS3535.E924 Z77 2001
813'.52--dc21
[B]
                                                              00-050261

Contents

H. A. Rey

H. A. Rey was born on September 16, 1898, in Hamburg, Germany. As a child, he liked to draw. He also liked to go to the zoo. Soon he was drawing animals.

In 1916, H. A. served in the German army during **World War I**. When he got out of the army, he went to college.

After college, H. A. moved to Rio de Janeiro, Brazil. He married Margret Waldstein in 1935. They started Brazil's first **advertising** company.

In 1936, the Reys moved to Paris. But they had to leave in 1940 during **World War II**. That year, they settled in New York.

In 1941, the Reys **published** a book about a monkey. It was called *Curious George*. Children loved Curious George. The Reys wrote many more books about him.

H. A. Rey died in 1977, and Margret died in 1996. But their books continue to delight children all over the world.

Opposite page: H. A. Rey

Growing Up

*H*ans Augusto Reyersbach was born on September 16, 1898, in Hamburg, Germany. His parents were Alexander and Martha Reyersbach. When he grew up, Hans changed his last name to Rey. As an adult, he was known as H. A. Rey.

H. A. spent his childhood like many children. He went to school. He played with his friends. He also loved to draw. He drew horses, trees, cars, and buildings. Sometimes, he drew during lessons in school!

H. A. lived near the Hagenbeck Zoo. He loved to see the animals. He watched how they moved and acted. H. A.'s love for drawing animals began at the Hagenbeck Zoo.

These monkeys live at the Hagenbeck Zoo.

A Student and a Soldier

*I*n school, H. A. studied reading, writing, and math. He also studied languages such as Latin, Greek, French, and English. He loved science, especially **astronomy**.

In 1916, H. A. was **drafted** into the German army. He served during **World War I**. H. A. served in the **infantry** and the medical **corps**.

H. A. was stationed in France and Russia. While in Russia, H. A. learned to speak Russian. He could speak six languages. In 1919, he was **discharged** from the service.

German soldiers in World War I

A New Job

*A*fter the war, H. A. went to college. He went to the University of Munich in 1919. In 1920, he went to the University of Hamburg.

In college, he studied science, literature, and languages. When he finished school, H. A. worked as an **illustrator**.

In 1924, H. A. moved to Rio de Janeiro, Brazil. Relatives there had offered him a job. He worked as an accountant. And he traveled along the Amazon River selling bathtubs and sinks.

H. A. worked as a salesman for 12 years. In 1935, he met Margret Waldstein. Margret was from Hamburg, Germany, too.

H. A. had met Margret in Hamburg at a party at her parents' house. Margret and H. A. liked each other. They began to date.

The University of Munich

Margret

*M*argret Waldstein was born in Hamburg in 1906. Her father was a member of the German **Parliament**. There were four other children in her family.

In 1927, Margret studied art at the Bauhaus, a **design** school in Dessau, Germany. In 1928, she studied at the Dusseldorf Academy. In 1930, she attended the University of Munich.

After she completed her studies, Margret worked in **advertising**. She wrote ads for products, such as soap. She also worked as a photographer and painted with watercolors.

In 1935, Margret moved to Rio de Janeiro. That August, she and H. A. Rey were married. In 1936, the Reys started Brazil's first advertising company. Later that year, they returned to Europe.

The Workshops Building at the Bauhaus

Escape from Paris

*T*he Reys moved to Paris, France. In Paris, H. A. worked on children's books. Margret helped him. In 1939, a company called Gallimard **published** H. A. Rey's first children's book, *Rafi et les Neuf Singes*.

That same year, Chatto and Windus published the English version of the book. It was called *Raffy and the Nine Monkeys*.

In 1940, the Reys had to leave Paris. **World War II** was raging in Europe. The German army was about to **invade** France.

In June 1940, the Reys left Paris. They took some food and a few books they were working on. They rode bicycles toward France's border with Spain.

When the Reys got to the border, they sold their bicycles. They took a train to Lisbon, Portugal. From there, they took a boat to Rio de Janeiro, and then to New York.

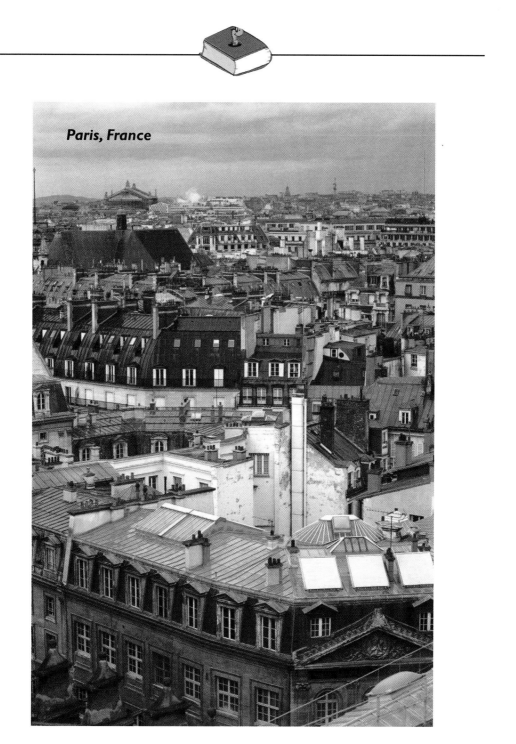

Paris, France

Curious George

*T*he Reys arrived in New York in October 1940. One of the books they brought with them was *Curious George*. They took it to Houghton Mifflin. *Curious George* was **published** in the United States in 1941.

In 1942, Chatto and Windus published *Curious George* in England. The book was called *Zozo*. At that time, George IV was king of England. The publisher did not want to **offend** the king or the English people. So Curious George's name was changed to Zozo for the English book.

Fans had to wait six years for the next Curious George book. *Curious George Takes a Job* was published in 1947. In 1960, it won the Lewis Carroll Shelf Award.

In 1966, *Curious George Goes to the Hospital* won the Children's Book Award by the Child Study Association of America. In 1987, *Curious George* won the *School Library Journal's* Children's Choice Awards prize as best picture book.

Curious George is also an American Library Association Notable Book.

   In all, the Reys wrote seven Curious George books before H. A. died in 1977. The other books were *Curious George Rides a Bike, Curious George Gets a Medal, Curious George Flies a Kite,* and *Curious George Learns the Alphabet.*

Margret Rey with Curious George

Other Books by the Reys

*T*he Reys created many books for children. H. A. worked on some of the books by himself. He and Margret worked on other books together. Sometimes they worked on other authors' books.

In 1942, H. A. used the **pen name** Uncle Gus. As Uncle Gus, he wrote *Christmas Manger*, *Uncle Gus's Farm*, and *Uncle Gus's Circus*.

H. A. also had many hobbies. He liked to read, swim, watch nature, and look at the stars. H. A. thought there should be a book that made identifying the **constellations** simple.

In 1952, he wrote a book about **astronomy** called *The Stars: A New Way to See Them*. In 1954, he wrote a children's book called *Find the Constellations*.

H. A. also **illustrated** books that other people wrote. In 1944, he illustrated *Katy No-Pocket*. It was a book about a kangaroo. In the book, Katy has a baby, but no pouch! Other popular books by the Reys are *Elizabite* and *Pretzel*.

H. A. and Margret Rey

Curious George Lives On

*I*n 1977, H. A. Rey died. Margret Rey died in 1996. But Curious George lives on. The first Curious George book came out more than 60 years ago. Today, all the Curious George books are still in print.

In 2000, Anita Silvey, the Reys' **editor** at Houghton Mifflin, visited the University of Southern Mississippi. She planned to open a show of the Reys' work in the de Grummond Children's Literature Collection.

While looking through the material, Silvey found a complete book called *Whiteblack the Penguin Sees the World*.

Silvey was excited. The Reys had written the book in Paris. It was one of the books they brought along when they came to New York. Houghton Mifflin **published** it in September 2000.

Today, Margret and H. A. Rey continue to delight audiences with their well-written and beautifully **illustrated** books.

Opposite page: H. A. Rey holds a monkey.

Glossary

advertise - to make or use public announcements to get people to buy things.

astronomy - the science that studies planets, stars, and other heavenly bodies.

constellation - a group of stars that forms a pattern shaped like an object, animal, or person.

corps - a military unit that has a certain function.

design - the art of making sketches, plans, and outlines that make a pattern for something.

discharge - to be released from military service.

draft - to be selected for military service.

editor - a person who makes sure a piece of writing has no errors before it is published.

illustrate - to make pictures and drawings to explain the words in a book. A person who does this is an illustrator.

infantry - soldiers trained and organized to fight on foot.

invade - to enter a country as an enemy and attack it.

offend - to cause anger or displeasure.

parliament - the highest lawmaking body in some governments.

pen name - a name an author uses that is different from his or her own.

publish - to produce printed materials for sale to the public.

World War I - 1914 to 1918, fought in Europe. The U.S., Great Britain, France, Russia, and their allies were on one side. Germany, Austria-Hungary, and their allies were on the other side. The war began when Archduke Ferdinand of Austria was assassinated. America joined the war in 1917 because Germany began attacking ships of countries that were not in the war.

World War II - 1939 to 1945, fought in Europe, Asia, and Africa. The U.S., France, Great Britain, the Soviet Union, and their allies were on one side. Germany, Italy, Japan, and their allies were on the other side. The war began when Germany invaded Poland. America entered the war in 1941 after Japan bombed Pearl Harbor, Hawaii.

Internet Sites

The World of Curious George Web Page!
http://www.georgeworld.com
Find out more information about H. A. and Margret Rey, play interactive games such as the Curious George Hat Game, send a friend a Curious George e-card, follow links to other Curious George Web sites, and more!

Curious George Virtual Tour
http://avatar.lib.usm.edu/~degrum/virtualtour/opener.htm
The de Grummond Children's Literature Collection presents a virtual tour of the Reys' life and work. Read more about H. A. and Margret's lives, see other works of art in other mediums, and get information on the de Grummond exhibit.

These sites are subject to change. Go to your favorite search engine and type in H. A. Rey for more sites.

Index